**Front cover cake
designed and created by**
Teresa Stewart

Back cover photo
Mark Vafiades

Special Thanks
Mell Flynn
Mark Vafiades

In honor of those who have lived long lives, and unknown to them, made the world a better place with positive, can-do, set-the-example-attitudes.

Stan Clothier 104
Peggy Bonan 100
Gordan in his 90's
Patricia Pyle
Aunt Jeanette in her 80's
And MANY more!

Copyright © 2024-2025 Story & Photography
Gale B. Nemec

All rights reserved. No part of this book may be copied or reproduced in any form or by electronic means, video, digital or mechanical, including information storage and retrieval systems, without written permission from the publisher, except for brief passages quoted in reviews.

ISBN 978-1-947608-26-9
Nemec Productions LLC
Alexandria, Virginia

This book belongs to

_____

This book is from

_____

Today's date

_____

I am over ninety!

Cannot believe it
is true.

But it dawned on me,

when others said,

(Drum roll. . .)

"Happy Birthday to YOU!"

I
may look old.
in your young eyes

*but the energy
and wisdom
I have
will give you a
Big Surprise!*

Yes, there are wrinkles, creaks and brown spots galore

*proof of my
long life,
a life I adore.*

For you see
teens,
20's,
30's,
40's,
50's
and
beyond.

*When you reach
my age
you will sing
this song.*

*"I am alive!
I made it!
How glorious
I am still here!*

God gave me another day on earth. I will cheer and I will cheer!"

*So...
When you
glance at me
and roll
your eyes,*

and see someone you think looks old

(A long drum roll. . .)

Here's another surprise!

*When I look
at you
and see
what you do,*

I pray, wish and hope

*you reach
my age, too.*

And that's my wish for you.

The End

Books, E-books, and Audible Books
Search Gale Nemec online

www.GaleNemecBooks.com
Email: Gale@GaleNemecBooks.com

Little Stockey & The Miracle of Christmas
There's A Bear on A Bench
The Great Elephant Rescue
Throwing Rocks in the River
No Valentines for Trevor or Emily
Valentines for Valentines Day
Trevor and the T's
Andy's Adventurous Nightmare
A Window into Heaven
Hugs
Hugs, Two photo book
Benjamin Loves the Beach
Santa's Gift drawing book for girls
Santa's Gift drawing book for boys
A Wish for You
God Held Your Hand

Bilingual: English Spanish
Hay un Oso En La Banca
(There's a Bear on A Bench)

El Pequeño Stockey y el Milagro de la Navidad
(Little Stockey & the Miracle of Christmas)

Non-Fiction
Caught in the Crosshairs of War

YouTube channel Gale Nemec
Your Song-The Ten Commandments Song

Interact with Gale reading these books on her YouTube channel:

There's a Bear on a Bench
Throwing Rocks in the River

PLEASE VISIT. LISTEN, LIKE AND SHARE.

Thank you for reading and buying this book. *Please* rate it on Amazon, Good Reads, Google and where you bought it with a star value or a written review. *Thank you.*

About the Author

Gale Nemec is an award-winning producer, actress, and voice talent. She is also a print model and song writer. Her most recent song
Your Song - The Ten Commandments Song
is on her
YouTube channel Gale Nemec,
and streaming platforms.

She created and produced *The Bea & the Bug* an award winning, multimedia, interactive musical show. She wrote and produced its theme song *You Can Make a Difference* and is currently working on a spin-off series *Adventures in Time*, a time-travel series for kids featuring American history.

Idea!

Write the name(s) of people who have lived long positive lives. You can name your list, *Positive Long Lifers*.
If you don't know anyone, write whatever you want to write, draw a picture, or leave this page blank. Share your list with me Gale@GaleNemecBooks.com

Positive Long Lifers

www.ingramcontent.com/pod-product-compliance
Lightning Source LLC
Chambersburg PA
CBHW041756040426
42446CB00001B/61